CREATURES
OF THE
ABYSS

BY SUE HAMILTON

Visit us at
WWW.ABDOPUBLISHING.COM

Published by ABDO Publishing Company, 8000 West 78th Street, Suite 310, Edina, Minnesota 55439.
Copyright ©2008 by Abdo Consulting Group, Inc. International copyrights reserved in all countries.
No part of this book may be reproduced in any form without written permission from the publisher.
Abdo & Daughters™ is a trademark and logo of ABDO Publishing Company.

Printed in the United States.

Editor: John Hamilton
Graphic Design: Sue Hamilton
Cover Design: Neil Klinepier
Cover Illustration: Diver and monstrous fish, ©2007 Rebecca Brace
Interior Photos and Illustrations: p 4 Anglerfish, Getty Images; p 5 Bathysphere, Corbis; p 6 Sperm whale, Getty Images; *Moby Dick* movie poster, courtesy Warner Brothers Pictures; p 7 Sperm whale and diver, Getty Images; p 8 Tortoise Tower, iStockphoto; Sea turtle, iStockphoto; p 9 George Wieland by archelon, Peabody Museum of Natural History, Yale University; p 10 The kraken from *Pirates of the Caribbean: Dead Man's Chest*, courtesy Walt Disney Studios; The Kraken postage stamp, courtesy Canada Post; p 11 French warship and giant squid, Corbis; p 12 Squid eye, iStockphoto; Squid beak, Photo Researchers, Inc.; Squid tentacles, iStockphoto; p 13 Colossal squid, p 14 Urquhart Castle on Loch Ness, iStockphoto; Swan, ©2006 Patrick Malycha; p 15 Plesiosaur, courtesy Brian Carter and the Smithsonian Institution's National Museum of Natural History; p 16 Surgeon's photo, AP Images; Submarine in Loch Ness, Getty Images; Researchers with sonar, Corbis; p 17 Loch Ness monster art, Photo Researchers, Inc.; pp 18-19 Sea monster, Corbis; pp 20-21 Lake sturgeon (top), courtesy Todd Kittel, College of Natural Resources, University of Wisconsin-Stevens Point; p 20 Lake sturgeon, courtesy Minnesota Department of Natural Resources; p 21 Lake Erie Monsters™ logo, photo courtesy and trademark of Cavaliers Hockey Holdings, LLC; p 22 Diver with eel monster, ©2007 Rebecca Brace; p 23 Diver and monstrous fish, ©2007 Rebecca Brace; p 24 Navy SEALs with oarfish, courtesy United States Navy; p 24 Oarfish illustration, Photo Researchers, Inc., p 25 Sea creature bones, AP Images; p 26 Dead basking shark, ©2006 Jonathan Riley; p 27 basking shark, Photo Researchers, Inc.; p 28 Coelacanth, Corbis; p 29 Diver photographing octopus, iStockphoto; p 32 *Creature From the Black Lagoon* poster, courtesy Universal Pictures.

Library of Congress Cataloging-in-Publication Data

Hamilton, Sue L., 1959-
  Creatures of the abyss / Sue Hamilton.
    p. cm. -- (Unsolved mysteries)
  ISBN 978-1-59928-836-9
  1. Sea monsters--Juvenile literature. I. Title.

QL89.2.S4H36 2008
001.944--dc22
                          2007014555

CONTENTS

Creatures of the Abyss 4

The Devil Whale 6

Snapping Terrors 8

The Kraken 10

Lake Monsters 14

Sea Serpents 22

Glossary 30

Index 32

CREATURES OF THE ABYSS

Above: The anglerfish is a deep-sea species. It lures its prey with a light on the end of its "fishing pole."

Earth's seas and oceans are places of great mystery. For hundreds of years, mankind could only guess what creatures lived in the world's watery depths. Sailors traveling through unexplored waters returned with stories of sea monsters. People living near deep, dark lakes sometimes saw unexplained creatures lurking in the water. Tales grew into legends. Facts became fiction. But many of these fictional stories did have some basis in truth.

Stories arose of such creatures as giant squids, dinosaur-age sea monsters, and fanged fish with evil eyes. People believed that any of these monsters would find a human quite a tasty snack. Some sea monsters were said to be big enough to drag down an entire ship, making the mysterious waters of the world both terrifying and incredibly interesting.

The urge to uncover the truth behind these creatures is very strong. Humans are too curious to be stopped by fearsome sea-monster stories, but our inability to breathe underwater did pose a rather large problem. Luckily, mankind has proven to be very inventive in finding ways to venture down into the depths. Around 100 A.D., hollow reeds were used as the first snorkels. In the 16th century, barrels became diving bells. The first submarines were built in the 18th and 19th centuries. These early subs were very dangerous. In 1771, John Smeaton invented the first air pump, allowing oxygen to be pumped down to divers. In the early 1930s, William Beebe and Otis Barton developed a bathysphere, a hollow steel ball that could be raised and lowered by a long cable attached to a ship.

In 1934, the two explorers dropped 3,028 feet (923 m) into the ocean, excitedly recording never-before-seen creatures that swam past their porthole. The window to the underwater world was finally opened.

Today's marine biologists and oceanographers use scuba diving gear, deep-sea submersibles, as well as sonar and radar to research Earth's depths. However, even with all our modern technology, there are still many questions to be answered. Do sea monsters exist? Are there areas where ancient sea creatures have survived the centuries? What unique species live in the holes, canyons, and trenches of our oceans? Answers to the unexplained mysteries of the creatures of the abyss are waiting out there. But what will we find?

Above: In 1934 marine biologist Dr. William Beebe and engineer Otis Barton invented the bathysphere. This device allowed them to dive deep into the sea, letting them view sea creatures that had never before been seen by humans.

THE DEVIL WHALE

Above:
Could a sperm whale, the largest of the world's toothed whales, have been mistaken for an island?
Below: A poster from the 1956 movie *Moby Dick*. Based on a story by Herman Melville, it is the tale of Captain Ahab and his unrelenting hunt for the great white whale, Moby Dick.

Is it possible that a sea creature could grow so big that it could be mistaken for an island? Saint Brendan, an Irish priest, claimed that he encountered just such a giant beast— the Devil Whale. The priest's frightening tale was written down in *The Voyage of Saint Brendan the Abbot.* During the 6th century, Brendan and 17 other monks ventured out onto the Atlantic Ocean in a small boat. One day they landed on a dark, treeless island, intending to build a fire and cook some meat.

When they approached the… island, the boat began to ground before they could reach its landing-place…The island was stony and without grass. There were a few pieces of driftwood on it, but no sand on its shore… the brothers began to carry the raw meat out of the boat to preserve it with salt.… When they had done this they put a pot over a fire. When, however, they were plying the fire with wood and the pot began to boil, the island began to be in motion like a wave. The brothers rushed to the boat… the island moved out to sea. The lighted fire could be seen over two miles away.

Brendan and the other monks escaped minus their food, but with their lives. The group returned home, telling people of their encounter with a fish of incredible size. They called it Jasconius, which became known as the Devil Whale.

Many theories about the mysterious and monstrous creature have been proposed. Some think it could have been a giant sea turtle, but most wonder if the great beast was in fact a sperm whale. A marine mammal, the grayish-black sperm whale reaches lengths of 60 feet (20 m). It is the largest toothed whale, and eats giant squid, octopus, and even sharks. (Other types of whales are baleen whales, which eat large quantities of plankton.) The famous Moby Dick, from Herman Melville's book, was a sperm whale.

Sperm whales often float motionless in the water, with just parts of their head and back showing. This is known as "logging." It is easy to approach a sperm whale when it's logging. Could a giant sperm whale, a creature weighing 40-50 tons (36-45 tonnes) have been the floating island that St. Brendan spoke of?

Below: A diver swims near a sperm whale.

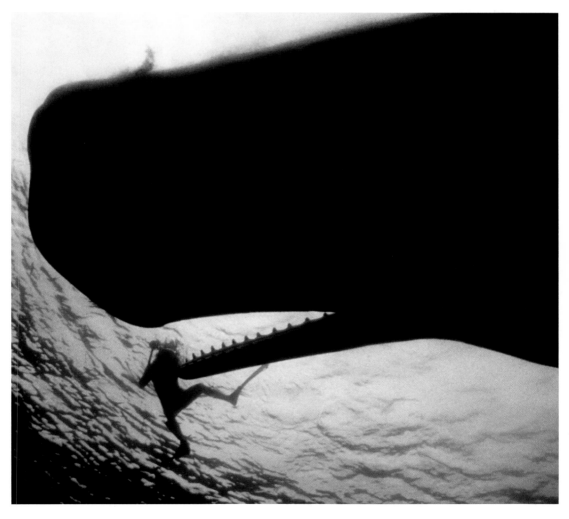

SNAPPING TERRORS

Above: Tortoise Tower in the Hoan Kiem Lake in Hanoi, Vietnam.

Archelon ischyros, or "large turtle," was the biggest turtle to swim Earth's oceans during the late Cretaceous period. It feasted on jellyfish and seaweed, and grew to the size of a small automobile. Its powerful hooked beak would have been strong enough to snap a human leg bone in two. Luckily, archelons died out 65 million years ago, long before humankind's appearance on Earth. Or did they?

Mysterious tales of gigantic sea turtles have been told for centuries. Sailors claimed that these creatures were so large that the turtles were sometimes mistaken for islands. Today's sea turtles are big, growing up to 7 feet (2 m), but not the monstrous size of the 15-foot (4.6-m) archelon. Is it possible some of these giant turtles are still alive?

Hoan Kiem Lake lies in the center of the bustling capital city of Hanoi, Vietnam. Within its waters lives a giant turtle, perhaps the last of its kind, and a legend in its own right. As the 15th-century story goes, King Le Loi was given a magic sword by the gods, which he used to defeat invaders to his land. One day, while cruising on the lake, the king was approached by a holy turtle.

Below: Today's sea turtles may grow as big as 7 feet (2 m), but ancient turtles reached sizes as big as a small car.

The turtle asked the emperor to return the magic sword to the gods, since peace had returned to the area. The sword flew into the turtle's mouth, and the great creature sank with it to the depths of the lake. From then on, the lake was known as Hoan Kiem Lake, or "Lake of Returned Sword."

Is the giant turtle of Hoan Kiem Lake the turtle of the story? No one knows, but turtles reportedly can live for hundreds of years, although most only live about 60 years. Could giant sea turtles have roamed our oceans, sharing the seas with the boats of our ancestors? Did archelons really become extinct, or are they still roaming our world? The mystery of the giant turtle remains, but people continue to search for the amazing creature.

Above: George Wieland stands by a nearly complete archelon fossil, which he found in 1895 in South Dakota. This specimen measures almost 11 feet (3.4 m) from snout to tail.

THE KRAKEN

Above: In 2006's *Pirates of the Caribbean: Dead Man's Chest,* the kraken attacked both merchantmen and pirate ships.

In ages past, sailors told of a squid-like monster so big it could reach up from the sea, wrap its tentacles around a ship, and draw the vessel and all aboard down to Davy Jones' Locker. Stories of this fearsome giant squid, called a kraken, were told for centuries. Author Jules Verne wrote about a giant squid attacking a submarine in his famous 1870 classic *Twenty Thousand Leagues Under the Sea*. In the 2006 film *Pirates of the Caribbean: Dead Man's Chest*, the kraken was called forth to attack sailing ships belonging to merchantmen and pirates.

Although once believed to be only a mythical creature, the giant squid, or *Architeuthis*, was discovered to be real in 1925. The proof included two tentacles found in a sperm whale's stomach. As time passed, additional species were found. The largest-measured giant squid was 60 feet (18 m) in length, but the average is 43 feet (13 m). Even an average-length giant squid is still a big monster. Imagine being a sailor or fisherman standing on the deck of a 100-foot (30-m) sailing ship and seeing a creature swim up to the boat whose body was half the length of the ship! Since the giant cephalopod rarely leaves its deep-sea home, it would likely be a once-in-a-lifetime, absolutely frightening experience.

Staring at the monstrous creature, sailors may have looked straight into the giant squid's eyes—the biggest of any living creature. Each one is about the size of a dinner plate, averaging 10 inches (25 cm) in diameter. Living in the deepest depths of the ocean, its huge eyes help it see its prey. Did it turn its eyes on the sailors, thinking it had found its next tasty snack?

Facing Page: An illustration showing the crew of a French warship attempting to catch a giant squid near Tenerife, one of the Canary Islands, in 1861. The crew was only able to retrieve part of the squid. *Below:* The kraken is on a 1990 stamp remembering legendary Canadian animals.

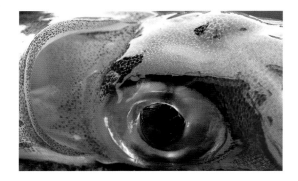

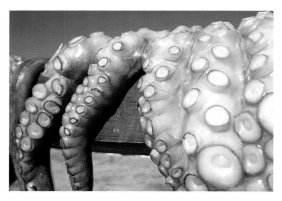

The giant squid's huge, parrot-like beak could easily tear a human apart. And even if the sailors tried to sail away, this squid is fast. It uses a type of natural jet propulsion to travel at speeds of up to 20 miles per hour (32 km/hr). It can even leap out of the water, launching itself at its prey or away from attackers.

There have been cases where a giant squid has attached itself to a smaller boat, perhaps mistaking it for something to eat. The long tentacle arms are covered with suction cups, which hold fast to its prey. It doesn't let go unless there's good reason. Sperm whales and Pacific sleeper sharks sometimes prey on giant squid, but even these fierce predators often bear the battle scars of the squid's tentacles.

How many colossal-sized squid roam the oceans? Where do kraken live? Modern science knows that giant squid do exist, although not to the size that ancient mariners reported. Were the tales simply exaggerations of the truth? Or are even greater creatures alive and waiting to be discovered?

It is still rare to see these creatures. When Japanese researchers filmed a live giant squid in December 2006, it made national news. Much of the kraken's mystery remains, but the answers lie in the dark depths of our oceans.

Left Top: A giant squid's eye is as big as a dinner plate.
Left Middle: A squid's parrot-like beak could easily tear a human apart.
Left Bottom: Squid tentacles hold tight to prey.

Above: In February 2007, a colossal squid was caught by New Zealand fishermen in the Ross Sea. It is thought to be the largest squid ever found anywhere in the world, weighing an estimated 992 pounds (450 kg). For centuries many people did not believe these huge mollusks were real, but in modern times the creatures have been filmed, as well as caught.

LAKE MONSTERS

Above: Urquhart Castle overlooks the deep waters of Loch Ness, Scotland.
Below: This out-of-focus picture looks like Nessie, but it's really a swan. It's easy to be fooled.

Almost everyone has heard of Scotland's famous Loch Ness monster, fondly referred to as "Nessie." But Nessie isn't the only mysterious creature that has been seen swimming in large lakes. Chesapeake Bay has "Chessie," a huge snake-like creature, seen by people living in Maryland and Virginia. And residents living along the shores of Lake Erie have reported sightings of "Bessie," a long, gray creature with a large head. Are these mysterious creatures real or mythical?

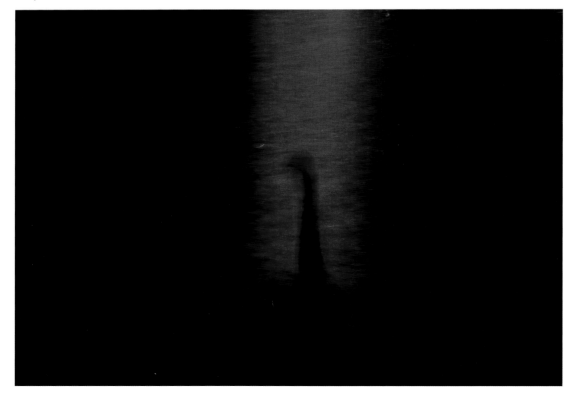

Nessie

The most famous lake monster of all is undoubtedly Scotland's Loch Ness monster. Nessie sightings have been reported for hundreds of years. Some believe the creature to be a plesiosaur, a long-extinct marine reptile that lived 200 million years ago. Scientific attempts to find the hidden creature are ongoing, despite the difficulty of searching such a huge lake.

Loch (lake) Ness is the largest fresh-water lake in Great Britain. It is 24 miles (39 km) long and up to 800 feet (244 m) deep. Its dark waters are filled with plankton, salmon, and other fish. It is the perfect hiding place for a shy aquatic creature.

Modern searches for the long-necked dinosaur with a small head and flippers began in the 1930s, when eyewitness accounts of the monster were reported in local newspapers, and then picked up by national media. However, uncovered hoaxes have caused many to believe that the Loch Ness monster is nothing but a figment of people's imagination.

Above: A short-necked plesiosaur or *Dolichorhynchops*, shown at the Smithsonian Institution's National Museum of Natural History in Washington, D.C. Some wonder if Scotland's Nessie is a plesiosaur survivor from the age of dinosaurs.

Above: The Surgeon's Photo, taken in 1934.

Above: A sub searched Loch Ness in 1969.

Above: Scientists searched for Nessie using sonar in 2001.

In 1933, big-game hunter Marmaduke Wetherell claimed that he had found sea-monster footprints along the shore of Loch Ness. Several months later, after studying plaster casts of the prints, scientists at the British Museum in London, England, correctly identified the imprints as being made from a dried hippo foot. Wetherell's trick was uncovered. Thoroughly embarrassed and publicly shamed, Wetherell wasn't finished with his Loch Ness foolery.

In April 1934, Dr. Robert Kenneth Wilson captured the Loch Ness monster on film. The Surgeon's Photo, as it came to be called, seemed to be proof that Nessie truly existed, although many scientists were still skeptical. They thought it was probably a photo of an otter or marine bird. Nearly 60 years later, the truth was finally revealed. Marmaduke Wetherell's stepson, Christian Spurling, confessed that the object in the photo was actually a toy submarine fitted with a clay sea-monster head. Spurling had helped the angry Wetherell create the photo, and Dr. Wilson, a prankster and a friend of a friend, had given the credibility needed to pull off the hoax.

What had been the biggest proof of Nessie's existence was all a fake. Still, searches continue for the mysterious creature. For decades, scientists and journalists have used the most modern techniques to search Loch Ness. Submarines equipped with sensing devices have canvassed the deep waters. Sonar, which detects objects under the water by sending out sound pulses and reading their reflected return signals, have produced images that looked like a giant flipper and the horned head of a creature. None of these clues, however, prove that Nessie lives.

Although many believe that the likelihood of finding the mysterious creature in Loch Ness is quite small, scientists insist on keeping an open mind. There is always the possibility that some type of prehistoric marine reptile actually exists. After all, new species of animals are found every year. Whether or not an actual monster lives in Loch Ness, people continue to research this fascinating unsolved mystery.

Above: Some people believe the Loch Ness monster is a hoax, but others are convinced that Nessie is a real creature.

17

Above: A serpentine sea monster that looks like the descriptions given of Chesapeake Bay's Chessie.

Chessie

Chesapeake Bay and its tributaries have had sightings of sea serpents since the mid-1800s. However, in the late 1970s and early 1980s, repeated reports of a giant snake-like creature caused officials and researchers to start paying attention. Nicknamed "Chessie" by the local media, the mysterious creature was described as 25 to 40 feet (8 to 12 m) in length, 8 to 10 inches (20 to 25 cm) in diameter, and possessing a football-shaped head. Unlike its Scottish cousin, however, witnesses said Chessie was serpentine—snakelike without fins or flippers. Also unlike the elusive Nessie, the Chesapeake Bay creature was actually captured on videotape in 1982.

On May 31, 1982, around 7:30 p.m., Robert Frew and his wife, Karen, spied a long, dark shape just offshore from their home on Chesapeake Bay. Robert grabbed his video camera and shot footage of the creature swimming toward a group of people in the water, diving under them, and then resurfacing on the other side.

The tape was shown to zoologist George Zug, as well as scientists from the Smithsonian Institution's National Museum of Natural History in Washington, D.C. Unfortunately, the quality of the video was too poor to allow researchers to determine exactly what was swimming in the water. In September 1982, following a great deal of publicity, scientists from Maryland's Johns Hopkins Applied Physics Laboratory offered to use their equipment and talents to enhance the quality of the video. Although they were able to determine that Chessie was definitely some sort of serpentine creature, money for the research ran out before the work could be completed.

Is Chessie a new species of giant eel, an unusually large snake, or a prehistoric creature once thought extinct? To this day, Chessie remains an unsolved mystery, but sightings continue to be reported.

Below: A lake sturgeon. Could the Lake Erie monster have been a large type of this fish?

Bessie/Lem

Lake Erie is the warmest of North America's Great Lakes, and the 11th largest lake on Earth by surface area. Along with fish such as sturgeon, walleyes, and trout, its waters appear to be home to a mysterious creature called South Bay Bessie.

Also known as "Lem" (which stands for Lake Erie monster), sightings of the water serpent in Lake Erie began as far back as July 1817. The crew of a schooner spotted a dark, reddish-brown, nearly black, 30- to 40-foot (9- to 12-m) -long creature. They did not know if it had scales, so it was impossible to guess if the creature was a snake or a fish, but some believed it might have been some type of gigantic eel.

Seventy years later, in May 1887, two brothers by the name of Dusseau told of finding "an unknown fish of mammal size." They beached the creature on the shore, where it seemed to die before their eyes. The brothers went to get something with

Below: Lake sturgeon grow to great sizes.

which to carry its body to their boat, but apparently it wasn't quite dead. The monster twisted back into the water and disappeared. All that was left were some immense, silver-dollar-sized scales.

Reports of a Lake Erie monster continued into the 20th century. During the 1980s and 1990s fishermen and boaters reported seeing some type of long, snake-like serpent lift its head out of the water.

Some swimmers were even attacked by a creature that left scratches and bite marks on their legs. This seemed to be proof that some kind of unknown marine animal was making its home in Lake Erie. However, when *The Beacon* newspaper in Port Clinton, Ohio, held a contest to name the creature, many people began to think South Bay Bessie was simply made up to draw in tourists. Still, a $150,000 reward was offered by businesses in nearby Huron, Ohio, for the "live and unharmed" capture of the serpent. A Lem/Bessie phone line was set up. Dozens of people called to report that they had seen a giant lake monster, and they were serious.

There is no doubt that the deep waters of Lake Erie have never been fully explored. Biologists and researchers have guessed that witnesses saw some kind of huge fish, like a sturgeon or bowfin, or perhaps an eel. However, a new, unidentified species could be out there, waiting to be found. And while the reward has officially been discontinued, the owner of the Huron Lagoons Marina has stated, "If anybody brought us a 30-footer weighing a thousand pounds, I think we'd still be willing to negotiate a large six-figure reward."

Below: The logo of the Lake Erie Monsters™, an American Hockey League team from Cleveland, Ohio.

SEA SERPENTS

Since people began sailing the world's oceans, brave sailors returned from their adventures with frightening tales of monstrous sea serpents. Mariners told of giant, never-before-seen creatures in a rainbow of green, black, brown, and gray colors. Various stories reported the sea creatures' sizes ranging from 20 feet (6 m) to a whopping 200 feet (60 m), over twice the size of a blue whale, the biggest mammal on earth. Sailors described the serpents as having a series of humps moving in an up-and-down motion. Some monsters were scaly, while others had smooth, rubbery skin.

Are sea serpents real? Or are they mythical creatures made up in the imaginations and fears of sailors?

Below: Imagine encountering a giant, eel-like sea serpent.

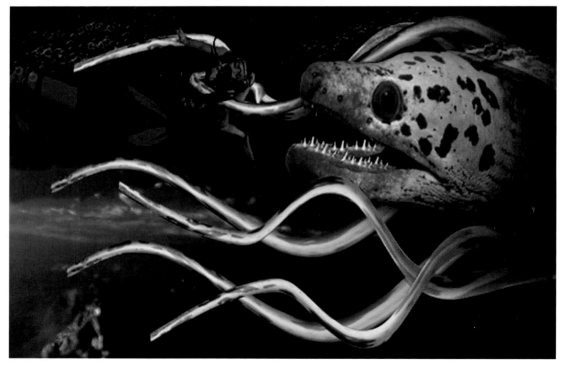

Above: Would you go in the water if the seas were filled with monstrous fish?

Above: In October 1996, Navy SEALs found this oarfish washed up on Silver Strand State Beach near Coronado, California. It was 24 feet (7.3 m) long and weighed 300 pounds (136 kg).
Below: An illustration of an oarfish.

Oarfish

Around 30 B.C., the Roman poet Virgil wrote that a Trojan priest and his two young sons were attacked by two huge sea snakes:

"Their fore-parts and their blood-red crests towered above the waves; the rest drove through the ocean behind, wreathing monstrous coils, and leaving a wake that roared and foamed. And now, with blazing and bloodshot eyes and tongues which flickered and licked their hissing mouths, they were on the beach."

Virgil's physical description of the creatures seems to point to the rarely seen, eel-like oarfish. This unusual deep-sea fish is silver, with a bright-red crest. It can reach lengths of up to 30 feet (9 m) and weigh up to 500 pounds (227 kg). It is quite shy, preferring to remain on the ocean floor, and surfacing only when it is sick or dying. Unlike Virgil's tale, it does not leave the water. However, since it is so rarely seen and is quite huge, it is easy to see how people could mistake it for a sea monster.

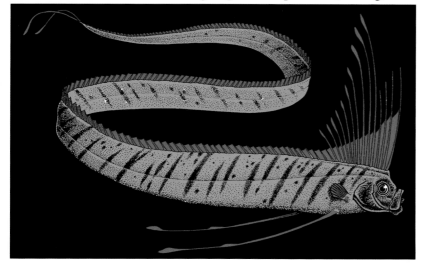

Basking Shark

In 1808, farmer John Peace saw a dead animal washed up on a rock near his home on Stronsay, an island that is part of the Orkney Islands in Scotland. He rowed out to take a closer look and discovered what appeared to be a hairy, 55-foot (17-m) sea monster. It had a long neck and tail, and five or six toes on each of its six feet. The face of the creature had been smashed, and Peace couldn't risk bringing his small boat any closer to the rocks for a better look. He rowed away wondering what really lay on the rock.

Right: The bones of an unidentified sea creature, nicknamed the "Block Ness monster," lies on the coast of Block Island, Rhode Island, in June 1996. Experts guessed that the 14-foot (4-m) skeleton could be the remains of a basking shark.

Below: A dead basking shark washed up on the shore of Nova Scotia, Canada, in 2006. The Stronsay beast was probably a rotting basking shark. As the fish decomposes, it could be confused for an unknown sea creature.

As luck would have it, a storm hit the area a few days later, bringing the beast's remains up on shore. An artist, Sir Alexander Gibson, was called in to sketch the creature, while another local man, George Sherar, measured and studied the carcass, taking careful notes.

News of the Stronsay beast spread across the country. The creature was named *Halsydrus,* or "sea water snake." Zoologists began to think an undiscovered creature had been found. However, when samples of the animal's skin and cartilage were examined by Sir Everard Home, the London doctor and naturalist knew that the mysterious creature was the rotting remains of a basking shark.

The second-largest fish after the whale shark, the basking shark can grow to some 40 feet (12 m) in length and weigh 16 tons (14.5 metric tons). Often spotted close to land, they are filter feeders, eating plankton and small fish.

Although now endangered from overfishing, they were once quite common, especially in the Orkney Islands, and often spotted near the water's surface.

With its pointed snout, huge 3-foot (.9-m) -wide mouth opening, and textured skin, basking sharks may have been responsible for many sea-monster sightings. In the case of the dead Stronsay beast, the scientists knew the monster's true identity by comparing it to a decaying basking shark. After it dies, the basking shark's jaw drops off, leaving what looks like a small head attached to a long neck. The body begins to rot, leaving the shark's spine to look like a long tail. The remains of the fish's fins look like legs, while the large top dorsal fin may have rotted to look like hairs.

It seems obvious that the mysterious and frightening Stronsay beast was simply the rotting remains of a common fish. Or was it? Even taking into account that the great fish had decayed, the fact remains that Stronsay's sea monster was quite a bit longer than the biggest known basking shark. Perhaps it is explainable, but the mystery continues.

Above: A basking shark filter feeds on plankton, showing its huge mouth.

Are there sea monsters and unknown creatures still swimming in Earth's oceans? The blue coelacanth, a fish once thought to have died out 80 million years ago, was discovered alive and swimming in 1938 off the coast of South Africa. Another coelacanth, a brown species, was found near Indonesia in 1998. A sea creature once believed extinct was found very much alive. If this "living fossil" could have survived the centuries, are other marine animals out there waiting to be discovered?

The fact is that many people have witnessed unexplainable sightings. From scientists and researchers to everyday people who live and work in and on our seas, oceans, lakes, and rivers, new marine species are found continually. The unsolved mysteries of the creatures of the abyss will likely remain as long as our waters hold life.

Below: A coelacanth, once thought to have died out 65 million years ago, is examined by scientists at the National Museum of Kenya in 2001. The fish was caught by local fishermen that same year.

Above: A diver researches and photographs an octopus.

GLOSSARY

CEPHALOPOD

A soft-bodied marine mollusk with a large head and eyes, a beaked mouth, and long arm-like tentacles attached to the creature's head. Cephalopod means "head foot," and includes squid, octopus, and cuttlefish. Most cephalopods eat fish, crustaceans, and other mollusks. Their tentacles are armed with rows of round suction-cup disks, which hold their prey. Fast swimmers, they propel themselves by forcefully shooting out water. Cephalopods also have an ink sac, which allows them to shoot out a cloud of dark fluid to help them escape from predators.

COELACANTH

Once thought to be extinct, this large, bony fish was found alive in the waters of the Comoro Islands near Madagascar in 1938.

CRETACEOUS PERIOD

A time period from about 146 million to 65 million years ago. The weather was warm, the first flowering plants grew, and dinosaurs lived throughout the world. The Cretaceous period ended with the abrupt extinction of the dinosaurs. The term Cretaceous comes from the Latin word *creta* which means "chalk." In 1822, Belgian geologist Jean d'Omalius d'Halloy named the era for the large amount of calcium carbonate, or chalk, that was deposited during that time by marine animals' shells. England's White Cliffs of Dover are an example of such deposits.

DAVY JONES' LOCKER

A centuries-old phrase of unknown origin meaning "the bottom of the ocean."

EXTINCT

An animal or species of animals that have no living members. Dinosaurs are extinct. Occasionally, creatures that were thought to be extinct have been found alive, such as the coelacanth.

MARINE BIOLOGIST

A person who studies animal and plant life in saltwater environments, such as oceans and seas.

OCEANOGRAPHER

A person who studies the ocean. This includes exploring the physical structure of the ocean floor, the ocean's water and currents, as well as the creatures living in the ocean.

RADAR

A way to find planes, ships, and other objects. Radar stands for **ra**dio **d**etection **a**nd **r**anging. The system sends out high-frequency electromagnetic waves, which bounce off any objects they hit, reflecting back to the source.

SCUBA

Scuba stands for **s**elf-**c**ontained **u**nderwater **b**reathing **a**pparatus. It is a device that allows divers to breath underwater for a certain period of time. Also know as an aqualung.

SONAR

A method of finding something submerged in water. A sonar device sends out sound waves and measures the time it takes for the echoes to return. The word comes from the phrase **so**und **na**vigation **r**anging.

SUBMERSIBLE

A small boat or vessel designed for deep-sea study and exploration. Some are unmanned, but contain lights, photo and video equipment, and various scientific instruments that can be controlled by a person on the surface. Manned submersibles are somewhat bigger, with a crew compartment, a pressure hull, and life-support systems that allow people to travel to the ocean floor.

TRIBUTARIES

Smaller rivers or streams that flow into a larger river or lake.

Right: A poster from 1954's *Creature From the Black Lagoon.* People wonder what sea creatures live in the dark depths of the earth's seas, oceans lakes, and rivers.

INDEX

A

Archelon ischyros 8, 9
Architeuthis 10
Atlantic Ocean 6

B

Barton, Otis 4
basking shark 25, 26, 27
Beacon, The 21
Beebe, William 4
Bessie 14, 20, 21
Brendan, Saint 6, 7
British Museum 16

C

cephalopod 10
Chesapeake Bay 14, 18
Chessie 14, 18, 19
coelacanth 28
Cretaceous period 6

D

Davy Jones' Locker 10
Devil Whale 6
Dusseau brothers 20

E

Earth 4, 8, 20, 28
England 16

F

Frew, Karen 18
Frew, Robert 18

G

Gibson, Alexander 26
Great Britain 15
Great Lakes 20

H

Halsydrus 26
Hanoi, Vietnam 8
Hoan Kiem Lake 8, 9
Home, Everard 26
Huron, OH 21
Huron Lagoons Marina 21

I

Indonesia 28

J

Jasconius 6
Johns Hopkins Applied Physics Laboratory 19

K

kraken 10, 12

L

Lake Erie 14, 20, 21
Lake Erie monster (*See* Lem)
Lake of Returned Sword 9
Le Loi (king) 8
Lem (Lake Erie monster) 20, 21
Loch Ness (lake) 15, 16, 17
Loch Ness monster 14, 15, 16
logging 7
London, England 16, 26

M

Maryland 14, 19
Melville, Herman 7
Moby Dick 7

N

National Museum of Natural History 19
Nessie 14, 15, 16, 17
North America 20

O

oarfish 24
Ohio 21
Orkney Islands 25, 27

P

Peace, John 25
Pirates of the Caribbean: Dead Man's Chest 10
plesiosaur 15
Port Clinton, OH 21

R

radar 5

S

Scotland 14, 15, 25
Sherar, George 26
Smeaton, John 4
Smithsonian Institution 19
sonar 5, 16
South Africa 28
South Bay Bessie (*See* Bessie)
sperm whale 7, 10

Spurling, Christian 16
Stronsay (island) 25, 27
Stronsay beast 26, 27
Surgeon's Photo 16

T

Twenty Thousand Leagues Under the Sea 10

V

Verne, Jules 10
Vietnam 8
Virgil (poet) 24
Virginia 14
Voyage of Saint Brendan the Abbot, The 6

W

Washington, D.C. 19
Wetherell, Marmaduke 16
Wilson, Robert Kenneth 16

Z

Zug, George 19